HOW TO:

ATTRACT MILLENNIALS TO YOUR COMPANY...

AND ACTUALLY KEEP US!

WRITTEN BY:

CAITLIN CROMMETT

CEO, FOUNDER

MILLENNIAL

Copyright © 2017 Caitlin Crommett

All rights reserved.

ISBN-10: 0-9981630-0-7

ISBN-13: 978-0-9981630-0-0

THANK YOU TO MY FAMILY, FRIENDS, MENTORS, AND EVERYONE WHO ASSURED ME THAT I ACTUALLY COULD WRITE A BOOK. I COULD NOT HAVE FINISHED THIS BOOK WITHOUT YOU.

AND THANK YOU TO ALL THE MILLENNIALS OUT THERE WHO ARE DOING GOOD FOR THE WORLD AND THOSE COMPANIES WHO ARE RECOGNIZING OUR ABILITY TO MAKE A DIFFERENCE.

CONTENTS:

INTRODUCTION — 11

CHAPTER 1: WHO ARE WE?! — 16

CHAPTER 2: WHO ARE YOU?! — 24

CHAPTER 3: YOU ARE WHAT YOU ATTRACT — 30

CHAPTER 4: WE'RE IN IT FOR US — 36

CHAPTER 5: THE SECRET IS TO WORK WITH US — 46

CHAPTER 6: WE ARE NATURAL ENTREPRENEURS — 53

CHAPTER 7: TECH, TECH, TECH — 65

CHAPTER 8: HEALTH ISN'T JUST PERSONAL — 72

CHAPTER 9: HOW WE WORK — 79

CHAPTER 10: WORKPLACE CULTURE AND ENVIRONMENT — 88

CHAPTER 11: WE WANT TO CHANGE THE WORLD — 95

CHAPTER 12: NOW THAT YOU'VE GOT US, KEEP US — 102

INTERVIEW WITH CHILI'S PRESIDENT — 111

INTERVIEW WITH ADROLL — 119

FINAL NOTES — 126

"Irrespective of the long-term aims and ambitions of an individual company, the ability to attract and retain Millennial talent will be a vital step to achieving it."
PricewaterhouseCoopers "Future of Work" Report

INTRODUCTORY NOTES

To begin, I'd like to say thank you. This is not an "Acknowledgements" page. Been there, done that. I want to thank YOU for caring about ensuring the future success of your company by bringing in the best new employees. And perhaps more importantly, keeping them there for the long term, despite the common notion that this Millennial generation is quite fickle.

Everyone is talking about how Millennials are so difficult to please, so caught up in their own lives, need to be rewarded, etc. etc. These are also the people that probably don't have any Millennials doing much for their companies, which might come back to bite them in the future.

Also, I'd like to make a clear correlation now between Millennials and the Baby Boomer generation. A generation ago, many people were calling the Boomers lazy, selfish, and other words that are now being used to describe Millennials. It seems pretty clear that people seem to enjoy labeling youth in their early to mid-twenties, which, as you may remember, is a very tumultuous, confusing time. This may be simply because twenty-somethings are quite selfish in general, or may seem this way because we are trying to figure out what we are doing with our lives while still wanting to have fun. Regardless, I will be making these connections to the Boomers throughout the book to show you how similar we truly are, and why we may actually be a match made in heaven for the workforce and beyond.

Back to the facts though, the real reason for writing this book today, and why it will help you **now**. The facts are this: **Millennials are now, beginning in 2016, the largest generation in the workforce.** See, wouldn't it make sense to try and attract not just any of those Millennials, but the BEST Millennials, to your company for the future? Hopefully you said yes to this, so you can keep reading. Otherwise, this book might not be of much use to you anymore. But if you're continuing on, thank you! This will be so fun.

Thank you for reading this book and recognizing that it has the potential to draw top people to your company. Coming from a Millennial, I'm fairly certain these tactics and strategies will draw the best of us, because you can be darn sure I've heard a bunch of my friends and colleagues complaining about their companies which are clearly not making this effort. You're ahead of the game, so kudos to you. Your future, and your company's future, is looking very bright from where I'm standing. Or maybe that's the empty glass I'm staring at as I type away in the coffee shop where I am surrounded by others of my same generation. Yes, it's true, we really do work in coffee shops. Strange, but good for you to know…

PERHAPS YOU'RE THINKING…WHO ARE *YOU* TO GIVE *ME* ADVICE?

Good question. I bet you were wondering who wrote this book you are about to spend a few hours of your life reading. Before I begin, I want to give you some background on me, Caitlin, and why in the world you would ever take my advice. Well, that is a great question.

Sure, I am still young. I just graduated from the University of Notre Dame and am 22 years old. But, that also means I am at the back end of my generation, the oh-so-famous Millennials. This means I have been able to observe and figure out why my friends, my older sister's friends, my mentors in my generation have taken certain jobs over others, why they have chosen to be with a certain company and not the other. I'm no Nancy Drew, but I've tried to figure out what everyone has in common, and the overwhelming concerns and desires held by Millennials I've encountered. I've been able to draw several conclusions from my detective work, so I will do my best to share what I have come up with so far.

On top of being the next Nancy Drew, I believe I can speak well for my generation, and here's why. But in all seriousness, I'm going to quickly go through what makes me a legitimate rep so you can fully trust me. I graduated in the top 3 of my high school class of over 800 students, and received the largest academic scholarship to Notre Dame that was offered. I started a nonprofit foundation at age 15, which I have now expanded to over 13 states. I have started 2 other organizations since then, making me a so-called "serial entrepreneur", and have received numerous achievement and leadership awards throughout my college years. Anyway, that is quite enough about me. I hope that will help establish some sort of credibility in your eyes as to why I can be a good representative of my generation, or at least the people in my generation that you might want working for you. Moving right along.

I am claiming to be a representative of my generation because of my experience with my generation, and my position right in the thick of those coming into the workforce- the people you want, NOW. Let me tell you right now that this book will not sugar-coat the facts- and I will not try and make my generation out to be something it is not. I take my responsibility as a (self-named) generational representative very seriously, and hope that you can find what you need in these next 12 chapters to take your company to the next level. So with that, let's get to the good stuff.

CHAPTER ONE: WHO ARE WE?!

"They are lazy, entitled narcissists who still live with their parents"- Joel Stein, TIME journalist, Gen X (age 45)

"[They] will entirely recast the image of youth from downbeat and alienated to upbeat and engaged- with potentially seismic consequences for America"- Neil Howe & William Strauss, authors on generational theory

"I think Millennials are a generation unlike anything we've ever seen on this planet"- Chelsea Krost, Millennial expert

We are Millennials! The greatest generation to ever live! Just kidding. But some may think so, with all of the advancements that have been made in our lifetime and the progress our country as a whole has made already- with new technologies and services like Facebook, Groupon, FourSquare, to name a few. These were all started by Millennials. And as a generation, we're barely out of our twenties. Some may think us to be the worst generation in history. I suppose it is all about perspective.

If you may recall, the Baby Boomers were quite similarly regarded as lazy, entitled, and demanding when they were in their early 20's. At the time, they were labeled as interested only in social change, distrustful of authority and government, and mockingly called the "Me" generation. Many felt disengaged with the world around them and horribly misunderstood. Well, look at them now! They are now viewed as productive, hard-working, and a generation that was so driven professionally that they sometimes forgot to take time to balance their work and family life. They have been a huge part of social change in this country, including the push toward civil rights, the feminist movement and the sexual revolution. They continue to have a huge impact on how the country runs, especially as they are beginning to move out of the work force and into retirement;

this is leaving many jobs open and creating the need for more healthcare options and leading to higher Social Security costs. These circumstances are causing ripple effects throughout the country and could create new obstacles for new workers to face when entering the workforce.

However, because many of the Boomers are so focused on their professional lives as I mentioned earlier, some continue to hold high positions in companies where Millennials are being hired. I hope that I can make it clear throughout the next chapters how well the two generations can work together, and why the combination might actually be the best ever. It is simply about taking advantage of this great partnership and how each can benefit and help the other.

Here's a quick preview of the Millennial generation before I dive into these topics and what they mean for your company in the next chapters:

WE ARE THE BIGGEST

Many do not realize that we have actually surpassed the massive Baby Boomer generation to become the largest generation in American history- we are 83.1 million strong, compared to the 75.4 million Boomers.[1]

You can take a moment to process that. I had to, that's for sure.

Yes, we are big. But being big doesn't mean that we feel any more understood than generations before us. We are criticized as being lazy but we think it's just because we have priorities more in tune with being young than lazy. But, you CAN figure out how to grab us early, and get the most out of us for your growing company. Never fear!

TECH-SAVVY!

Yes, this one is quite obvious. We are tech-obsessed. We grew up with cell phones in our hands and computers on our laps. We have had our coming of age in the new millennium- hence our name- which has been the most technologically advanced in history. We can't imagine a world without Internet and WiFi. If you want to appeal to us, make sure you have your technology up to date and incorporated into your company. Even if your company is literally a paper-making or pen distribution company, still pushing the power of pen and paper... You must have technology. That is a huge priority. I don't want to sugar-coat anything, so I just need to make sure we all understand how crucial it is to make the effort to have updated technology in your office. Yes, I understand that some companies cannot afford to invest huge dollars in technology, so company goals that incorporate tech into the workplace will go a long way toward showing your Millennial prospects that you "get it", but just can't afford it all yet. It's the thought that counts.

SOCIAL BUTTERFLIES

I'm not saying that we are all outgoing extroverts; that would be quite an overload of talkative people. But rather, I am saying that we are largely all socially-minded and socially-driven. Social media is a constant in our daily lives. We rely on reviews from friends and word of mouth to get our information. We like our feedback in real time, from a real person, and not in a packed Excel report. We appreciate human interaction, in any form, when it comes to making decisions in our lives. This may seem counter-intuitive, if you look at the many in our generation who seem to always be looking at our phones rather than the people in front of us. But these two concepts can, in fact, peacefully coexist. We love the technology and connection our phones offer, but appreciate even more the effort of human interaction when it comes to our workplace- it feels more personal, when we are used to the impersonal lives we connect to on our devices.

Gone are the days of individual decision-making. These are the days of, "what do you think of this new hair color before I try it" posts on Facebook or "what do you think of this company before I accept the offer" group texts. We rely on our friends, family, and classmates to assist with our decisions. Yeah, it may seem obnoxious to you independent-thinkers, you Boomers who decided things on your own as young people. But as Boomers are rapidly changing into mentors and teachers, our two cultures will mesh perfectly. We want personal interaction and the Boomers are now ready and willing to offer it. I suppose times they are a'changin', and I hope you can accept our strange new ways.

WE LIKE TO START THINGS

Like I mentioned earlier, I consider myself a serial entrepreneur. And that is pretty common for someone of my age because we are obsessed with starting things. We have grown up with the mentality that "anything is possible", drawing from the crazy Mark Zuckerburg success stories surrounding us, feeding us with a drive to create our own futures, much like the Bill Gates and Microsoft success story that surrounded Boomers when they were entering the workforce. But, don't worry, this doesn't mean we won't want to work for you. Stay tuned for how to capitalize upon our entrepreneurial spirits.

WE BASICALLY WANT TO CHANGE THE WORLD
BOOMERS: THIS SHOULD ALL SOUND VERY FAMILIAR TO YOU. READ ON.

Whether it is with our own company or with your company, we want to be a part of a big, awesome change. Or really anything that will make the world better because of it. If it might not be the product you are selling or the service you are offering, we want to know you still care about something bigger than you and your company. Sure, you may refer to this as the "optimism of youth", but to us it is bigger than that. We believe it will continue far past our youth.

As an example, a friend of mine was willing to work on a movie for free, to learn and gain experience over the course of the production. But, once this position turned into one where she was simply running silly errands and no longer learning or meeting people, she drew the line. She demanded that she be growing and learning if she is giving her time up for free, something that is crucial to many of us, no matter how passionate about the project.

The world has changed in huge ways as we have grown up; we are in a world where equality is expected, and change is inevitable. We've seen people close to us lose jobs in a suffering job market, the instability of the economy, the rich get richer as others suffer, the beginning of driver-less cars and artificial intelligence. We have become accustomed to constant progress, and we want to know that you are into it too. If you are a Boomer, you probably understand this part of us quite well…so that makes things easier.

CHAPTER 2:

WHO ARE YOU?!

"The day you find out who you are is when you look back and realize that it was never the words, rather your actions that defined you." Shannon L. Alder, author

While unfortunately I cannot yet look from the page to the reader and personally examine who you are (we perhaps will get there at some point at this rate!), I am going to assume a few things, if that's okay. I am making these assumptions because sometimes we are not even fully aware of who or what we are in certain cases, and I think it is important that we quickly set that straight before continuing.

It is quite likely that you are a Baby Boomer or Gen X member looking for guidance in managing this new generation in the workforce, the evasive Millennials. This book is largely geared to those in management positions because of the nature of the relationship with your Millennial employees that I refer to in this book. If you are in fact a Boomer, you will find that you can probably relate to much of what is said in this book because our generations are actually more similar than we think. And, you will learn that we are primed to work together perfectly and may in fact be a match made in heaven. See page 28-29 for a more detailed analysis of our generations side-by-side.

YOU ARE FUTURE-ORIENTED

You clearly want to get on top of the trends, know things before your friends or colleagues, and basically just stay ahead. You would not be reading this book if this were not your mindset, because it is clear that the Millennials are the future of America, for now. In this day and age, being obsessed with the future and the approaching trends is the only thing that will give you a competitive advantage every time. You read your industry-specific articles, you watch the news online, you browse the Internet on your breaks looking for the next upcoming "big thing". And even if you don't do all these things yet, you soon will, because you will have a bunch of eager Millennials knocking on your door for a job who will be glad to impart their tech-wisdom upon you.

INNOVATION IS YOUR FAVORITE BUZZ WORD

It's such a nice word isn't it? Make sure to keep using it, because we may love that word more than you. In fact, we may choose your company just because you say you encourage and promote innovation; 66% of us say it is critical requirement in choosing a potential employer.[2] That's a whole lot of people that like that word, and I'll help you figure out how to make sure that is clearly in your ideals as a company.

YOU ENCOURAGE AND ACCEPT CHANGE

Some companies are just stuck in a rut because their management is afraid of change and what it might do to their profits, shares, etc. I might be out of my right mind, but I think positive change and innovation *is the actual vehicle* that could increase profits and growth on a massive level! But, some may not fully agree, so I will attempt to explain myself at some point later, to try and help you understand our mindset a bit more. At least we know you are all about change, and willing to do what it takes to improve your company for the future. So let's get started on some big changes and getting your company to where it can, and should, be in the coming years.

GENERATIONAL COMPARISONS IN THE WORKPLACE

BABY BOOMERS

"Me" Generation

Previous generations see us as: Rebellious

Optimistic

Tend to work long hours, value work ethic

Learned and acquired technological skills

Skeptical of authority, now becoming traditionalists

Time and experience should correlate with authority

Organizational hierarchy

Work is a Career

Look for career where I can make a difference

Do well in teams, team players

Love praise, feel rewarded by money, awards

Want to be mentors to younger employees

MILLENNIALS

Generation Next

Previous generations see us as: Entitled

Optimistic

Tend to multitask & work flexibly, value ambition

Born with technology, integral to life

Challenge authority, but seek out guidance

Skill and contribution should correlate with authority

Collaborative, equal work environment

Work is Fulfillment

Look for a career where I will grow and learn

Thrive in a team-oriented workplace, participative

Love feedback, want recognition for job well done

Want mentors who have guidance to offer

CHAPTER 3:
YOU ARE WHAT YOU ATTRACT

"The world is a great mirror. It reflects back to you what you are. If you are loving, if you are friendly, if you are helpful, the world will prove to be loving and friendly and helpful in return. The world is what you are." ~ Thomas Dreier, author

Let's start with the basics. Who or what do you want to be as a company? What kinds of people do you want working for you? For instance, if you are a super-cool, hip, smart, trendy company, you are going to attract a lot of those kinds of people. A lot of the big tech companies clearly attract certain types of people, as they exude that same image of who would fit in there. Culture and image really make a difference when it comes to attracting Millennials. Let's review what this means for you.

MAKE YOURSELF CLEAR

If you don't already know, make sure you have a clear idea of not only what you want your company to be, but also **who** you want it to be. If you are a tech company, for example, you could be the smartest, quickest company with a slight "nerdy" reputation- perhaps like Geeksquad. Their brand is in their name. If you're a bank, you could stick to the typical bank "image" of suits, ties, corporate offices, and large conference rooms. Or, you could get a little creative and use a more modern approach with open conference rooms, glass walls, more casual attire, and more creativity encouraged. But just to add a bit of perspective here, a recent article has said that 71% of Millennials would prefer to go to the dentist over a bank.[3] Why? Simply because of the inefficiency and lack of freedom that it presents, especially when compared to the ease of recent financial applications like Venmo and Apple Pay. They would rather deal with money online, instead of waiting in line and taking time at a bank to deal with money matters.

Each of these images of a company will attract different people to come work for you, so you need to be clear on the kinds of people you want working for you, and what they could bring to the future of your company in a changing world.

Corporate culture starts with you and the other leaders in your company. If you are clear in communicating your culture to Millennial prospects, you will turn some of them away from you because they are seeking something else. But, you haven't wasted time training them only to have them leave because the company doesn't match up with their cultural or social expectations. Might as well get some things straight right off the bat!

EXUDE YOUR IMAGE PROPERLY

Sometimes companies might get caught up in this idea of "image" and put too much time and energy into it before really understanding how to properly act on it. This is precisely where they go wrong. Exuding the appropriate image is dependent on the people in the company, the culture you promote, and the activities you promise.

Sure, a company can claim to be "socially responsible" and work hard to attract the people who care most about this aspect, but this will not get them anywhere if they aren't truly dedicated to the idea. Millennials need to see that you are *doing something* about the things you claim are important to you, and not just throwing money at them or saying you are going to do them in the future.

For example, don't say you are actively involved in your local community if all you do is organize an annual company fundraiser for United Way. Sure, fundraisers are great, helpful and necessary, but the involvement is not on par with the real "get-your-hands-dirty" mindset of most Millennial volunteers. If your employees are volunteering at local United Way chapters and you are rewarding and recognizing them for their efforts, now that's local community involvement.

You must remember, we are a generation of Doers, so we want to see things get done. And usually, we can see if you are making a difference in any real way because of our reliance on reviews and what people tell us, and of course our Nancy Drew-like detective skills as mentioned earlier.

GET SEEN

Remember my whole focus on *social* earlier? Well the same applies here; we want to be able to share cool photos with our friends or interesting articles about something our company is doing. We want to show off that we are part of something cool. Make sure your social media outlets are in place so that we can be sure to see the things you are doing, even before we get there.

If you're worried that the potential for causing distractions at work outweighs any other social media benefits, think again. We love to share things we think are cool on our social media pages, and if we can do that with something at our own work, where we are every day, think of the potential for creating company pride amongst your workers. In the long term, this could increase your employee retention rates, because we feel more connected and proud of the place we work, rather than it being something we can't even talk about on our main form of online communication- social media.

Most companies today have a social media manager of some sort, simply because of the importance that today's world places on image and public exposure online. If you are able to incorporate this position somehow into your company, it will be in your best interests to strategically post and represent yourself in a way that is aligned with your company culture. Some companies aim toward certain audiences, and thus must shift their social media and online exposure to attract that audience. For example, if you are a travel company with the intended audience of a young person looking for a cheap fun vacation, you would post on social media (probably Instagram) things like: articles and photos of the best new hostels, the cheapest bus routes, the best cities for nightlife. If, however, you want to be seen as a luxury travel company, you would post articles (probably on Facebook) about the Ritz Carlton, first class travel, and luxury restaurants around the world. See where I'm going with this? You can decide who you want to attract, who you want to become, as a company, but be sure to get seen on social media in that same image so as to remain consistent and targeted. Now, go post on social media with this in mind….I'll wait!

CHAPTER 4:

WE'RE IN IT FOR US

We do have a sense of entitlement, a sense of ownership, because, after all, this is the world we were born into, and we are responsible for it." -Evan Spiegel, CEO Snapchat, Millennial

No, I do not mean we are selfish. We are far from it, with our obsession with social change, civil equality, and changing the world for the better. I'll get into that later, but I assure you most of us are largely, if not solely, motivated by what we can do to make the world a better place in our lifetime.

But, when it comes to our careers, we are certainly quite motivated toward success and we will stop at nothing to get to our goals. And I hate to say it, but your company might just be a stepping stone for us on our way to the top of our personal mountain. However, if you use this book wisely, you might just figure out how to keep us and adjust our mountains to include your company at the top.

KNOW OUR MINDSET

This will help you beyond any other piece of advice I could offer. Knowing what we are thinking when we enter your company might just allow you to gradually change what we are thinking. I realize how this might sound- self-centered, maybe, narcissistic, sure. We've been called that our entire lives, as a generation; similar to the Boomers back when they were younger as I mentioned earlier. But realistically, we know that each company we work with is simply a stepping stone to our goals. Especially right out of college, we go in with the mindset that we will most likely leave within a few years.

Your company will provide us great leverage to get to our next goal, which may be more in line with our personal passions. If you know this right off the bat, you can help us advance and grow within and outside of your company, giving us less and less reason to want to leave. You may even tell us that you are aware we are still in the early stages of our careers, and that you hope to help us grow and learn as much as possible while we are with you. That would be a dream to hear, speaking from personal experience, and might help you immensely in the future while working with us. The common understanding that Millennials prefer to jump around between companies rather than sticking with one could be avoided if you are to better understand our desire to grow. Employers want loyalty, Millennials want growth. This could be a mutually beneficial relationship if properly addressed early.

Keep in mind, though, that we value sincerity and if you are to say these things to us and make promises, we would love for you to actually follow-through. If, for example, you say you want to help expand my foundation, DreamCatchers, by supporting its efforts within the company, that is a great start.

(Quick side-note here: My foundation, DreamCatchers, is dedicated to fulfilling the final Dreams of hospice patients, who are people diagnosed with a terminal condition and given 6 months or less to live. You can find out more at www.dreamcatchers1.org).

But follow-through is crucial- please do not consistently brush off my ideas on how we can incorporate mutually beneficial concepts into the workplace. A company-wide fundraiser, organization of a fair to support the charity, or even a company day at a hospice to help raise awareness- these are all perfect examples of enthusiastic engagement and commitment to supporting the foundation. If you want to work together and say that, then we expect you to be sincere and not just saying things to please us. Speaking from experience, I know that this is something we will remember, whether you stick to your word or not. And you might have a better chance of keeping us for the long haul, if this kind of engagement and commitment occurs regularly...

WE WANT TO GROW

As I mentioned earlier, each step in our careers is a chance to grow and learn more than we have before, and you need to be aware of our desire to continue this growth wherever we go. In a recent survey, 65% of Millennials said that the opportunity for personal development was the most influential factor in their current job.[4]

If you know this and help us with this development, then we will feel more inclined to stick with you to continue in our own growth. As soon as our development and learning becomes stagnant within a company, we are already planning our exit strategy. And if you're wondering how to promote this within your company and turn this advice into action, turn to some of the top companies in this area, like GE.

CASE STUDY: GENERAL ELECTRIC[5]

GENERAL ELECTRIC (GE) PLACES A HUGE EMPHASIS ON LEADERSHIP DEVELOPMENT, PREPARING EMPLOYEES FOR THE FUTURE THAT THEIR CAREER CAN HOLD. THE COMPANY HAS BEEN RANKED THE TOP COMPANY IN AMERICA FOR LEADERS, DUE TO ITS EMPHASIS ON EMPLOYEE DEVELOPMENT AND PROMOTION.

HOW:

GE SPENDS $1 BILLION PER YEAR ON EMPLOYEE DEVELOPMENT ALONE, SOMETHING THAT THEY HAVE CLAIMED TO BE INTEGRAL TO THEIR CULTURE SINCE THE BEGINNING. THE TOP LEADERS IN THE COMPANY SPEND OVER ONE-THIRD OF THEIR TIME ON LEADERSHIP

DEVELOPMENT, AND PREPARING THEIR EMPLOYEES TO BE AT THE TOP. GE EVEN HAS A COMPANY CORPORATE UNIVERSITY IN CROTONVILLE, NEW YORK, WHICH HAS BECOME A GLOBAL HUB FOR THINKING ABOUT LEADERSHIP, INNOVATION, STRATEGY, AND PERFORMANCE. THE COMPANY PROVIDES COURSES ON LEADERSHIP AND DEVELOPMENT FOR EMPLOYEES, BOTH ON THIS CAMPUS AND ONLINE FOR GREATER FUNCTIONALITY. THERE ARE VARIOUS LEVELS OF COURSES- ONLINE, THE CROTONVILLE CAMPUS, AND EVEN A REMOTE FACILITY FOR A MORE INTENSIVE WEEK-LONG LEADERSHIP COURSE WHICH HAPPENS THROUGHOUT AN EMPLOYEE'S FIRST TEN YEARS WITH THE COMPANY. GE CONTINUES TO OFFER COURSES UP TO THE EXECUTIVE LEVEL, GIVING EVERYONE AT EVERY LEVEL THE OPPORTUNITY TO HONE THEIR LEADERSHIP AND TECHNICAL SKILLS NECESSARY TO MOVE UP IN THE COMPANY.

WHAT YOU CAN DO:

- Ensure that your top leaders impart their wisdom regularly on their mentees, and that no one moves on from their position without ensuring there is a proper leader to take their place; preferably an internally "developed" leader.

- Small and larger companies must ensure that communication lines are open, and development strategies are in place. If you are smaller, assign mentors to newer employees that they can rely on regularly. If you are larger, like GE, it is crucial to establish relationships that can last and make the environment feel tighter, much like the feeling of a smaller company. This way, leaders are likely to come from within a strong mentor/mentee relationship.
- Talking, training, mentoring, communicating are important regardless of size.
- Provide lots of opportunities for personal development- send employees to useful conventions to learn new skills, host leadership training courses, provide on-line learning capabilities, continually add responsibility and leverage to their position, etc. Tie all of these tips together and create a "Employee Highlight" section on your website when an employee submits an awesome takeaway from their last convention. They'll feel important, which will boost their loyalty to you. Let us

share it on social media for all of our friends to see our website feature- bonus points for you!
- Even if you are strained financially and can't offer structured programs right now, you can have a brown-bag lunch session every month for employees to brainstorm ideas, discuss leadership, shoot down rumors, etc. Being active in the everyday lives of all employees goes a long way in our world.
- Host **focus groups** to receive feedback from your leaders and future leaders, to better understand what they would like to see changed in the company. Follow up on the results, even if it is simply to say that you won't be implementing something. Better to say no to a project than to ignore it.

FOCUS GROUPS AND FEEDBACK TIPS

EFFECTIVE FOCUS GROUPS CAN DO WONDERS FOR A COMPANY AND ITS INTERNAL DEVELOPMENT. TO HELP YOU GET STARTED WITH THIS SUGGESTION, I RECOMMEND GATHERING A GROUP OF NEW EMPLOYEES, IN ALL DIFFERENT SECTORS OF YOUR COMPANY. APPOINT A NEUTRAL LEADER, ONE FROM A SECTOR THAT IS NOT REPRESENTED. GUIDE THE DISCUSSION TO FOCUS ON THEIR DAILY TASKS AND WHAT

THEY LIKE, DISLIKE, WHAT THEY FEEL COULD BE IMPROVED UPON. MAKE SURE IT IS A SAFE SPACE, WHERE THEY FEEL THEY CAN SHARE THEIR SUGGESTIONS OPENLY AND THEIR DISLIKES FREELY WITHOUT CONSEQUENCE. THEN, ROTATE GROUP STRUCTURE TO INCLUDE MEMBERS OF THE SAME SECTOR, WHO CAN THEN COLLABORATE TO FOCUS ON WHAT COULD BE IMPROVED UPON FOR THEIR SECTOR ONLY. GIVE THEM THE TOPICS IN ADVANCE, SO THAT THEY CAN THINK ABOUT THEM AS THEY WORK AND WILL THUS SEE ISSUES IN REAL TIME.

OTHER EFFECTIVE FEEDBACK METHODS CAN BE CONSTANTLY DEVELOPED TO ENSURE THAT EMPLOYEES ARE HAPPY AND FEEL THAT THEIR COMPANY LISTENS TO THEM:

SET UP AN ANONYMOUS SUGGESTION/COMPLAINT/"SNAPS" BOX WHERE EMPLOYEES CAN DROP-IN THEIR THOUGHTS AT ANY TIME. AT THE END OF EACH WEEK, OR DURING A COMPANY-WIDE MEETING, READ EACH COMMENT ALOUD, AND TALK THROUGH WHAT COULD BE DONE TO IMPROVE IT, ADDRESS IT, OR SIMPLY "SNAP" FOR ANYTHING GOOD THINGS THAT SHOW UP IN THERE. YOU WILL SHOW US THAT YOU WANT TO IMPROVE, AND YOU WANT EVERYONE TO BE ABLE TO SHARE THEIR THOUGHTS IN A SAFE ENVIRONMENT. OR, SEND OUT AN EMAIL NEWSLETTER AT THE END OF EACH WEEK FILLING US ALL IN ON WHAT HAS BEEN GOING ON WITH

MANAGEMENT THAT WEEK, ANY UPDATES THAT AFFECT THE EMPLOYEES, ETC. WE WANT TO STAY IN THE LOOP, SO WE KNOW HOW WE ARE SPENDING OUR TIME ON EACH DAY FITS INTO THE BIG PICTURE.

CHAPTER 5:

THE SECRET IS TO WORK WITH US

"In most cases being a good boss means hiring talented people and then getting out of their way." -Tina Fey, actor, comedian

Gone are the days of only working "for" your boss. Boomers intuitively understood this in their disdain for authority and this mindset is now firmly established in corporate America. Again, the Boomers led the way on this concept and now Millennials expect it to be understood by employers. Today, we expect to be working WITH our bosses, our supervisors, and whoever may be theoretically "above" us in the system to get the job done. This way, there are no barriers to getting things done at the highest levels, on the largest scale.

"With [Milennials] coming into the business, hierarchies have to disappear. [Millennials] expect to work in communities of mutual interest and passion - not structured hierarchies. Consequently, people-management strategies will have to change so that they look more like Facebook and less like the pyramid structures we are used to."

Vineet Nayar Vice Chairman and CEO, HCL Technologies, India

On that note, hierarchical corporate structures are also not high on our list of favorite things. Millennials are fond of a less structured, less pyramid-like workplace, one where everyone can feel equal. See "Workplace Culture and Environment" on page 88 for more ideas on how to achieve this by adjusting your office space.

WHY?:

This way, we will not feel "below" anyone at work, which fosters a feeling of inferiority and thus stifles creativity and innovation. Wouldn't it be perfect if we could just nudge the person sitting next to us with a cool idea that pops into our head, and it happens to be our supervisor who can actually help us take it to fruition? That is to assume we are actually in the office, and not working from home on one of our mobile office days- I will get into this later.

Many respond well to mentoring by older employees - in an ideal world, they would like to see their boss as a coach who supports them in their personal development - but also generally prefer to learn by doing rather than by being told what to do.[6]

This speaks perfectly to the exciting new revelation that Boomers and Millennials may in fact make perfect teams in the office. Boomers have had decades of learning new skills, so are wired for what works, and also are at the point where they want to see their knowledge passed on and put to use in the future.[7] Millennials, coincidentally, want mentors who can guide them and explain what to avoid to make the best progress and biggest contributions. Viola! A match made in heaven. I personally know many Millennials who rave about their supervisors and bosses who have become genuinely interested in both their career progression and their passions outside of work. This sense of connectedness fosters the belief that the boss is truly concerned with the overall success of the employee, personally and professionally.

HOW?:

I will attempt to offer some suggestions for how to best go about making your employees feel more comfortable and equal in the workplace. Of course, there are many opportunities for other methods, but these are personal favorites from experience and stories from friends, so thought I would share them with you now. Take it or leave it, as always!

STEP 1:

Some tips from personal observations and research on how to make us feel like you are on our level: When we come in for an interview, sit on the same side of the desk as us. Often times people will have two chairs behind their desk, or even a little sitting area where there is no separation. This will create a foundation for our relationship with one another, showing us that you are in fact "on our side", and want us to feel as though you are a coworker rather than the "big boss" who we are naturally a bit afraid to approach. The desk almost becomes a symbolic barrier, and it would be better to eliminate that right away the first time we meet you.

STEP 2:

Correct us when we use a prefix before your name. I think you may have suspected this one was coming. The days of "Mister" and "Misses" are coming to an end, in many cases. Don't get me wrong, most of us will still use it as a natural reaction until we are told otherwise. With workplaces becoming more casual, and the preferred notion of working on the same playing field as supervisors, it just makes sense to have that carry over into names and addressing coworkers and bosses. Have us greet you with your first name, or even a nickname should you prefer it, so that we feel even closer to you in position, or even simply more comfortable with you as a person we would spend time with daily. This will relax our relationship with you, and we will in turn be more inclined to come to you with ideas directly and work harder *with* you.

"My company is chill- they told us to call everyone by their first names, even the CEO, on the first day. I think it simplifies things and makes everyone more approachable"- Carly, Advantage Marketing Solutions

STEP 3:

If you're out of ideas or these don't work as well for you, there's always the simple, straightforward solution. Tell us straight up: "You work WITH me, not FOR me." I'd say that would get the message across pretty quickly. We would appreciate that, I bet we would even tell our friends how cool you are because of the way you are treating us and speaking to us right away. This breaks the barrier that we were hoping wasn't going to be there, and helps us to know that we can treat you as an equal rather than a superior. Sure, superior-inferior relationships work well in certain situations, perhaps in an Army platoon for example. But in your situation, which is probably a management-level or managerial department of some sort, people like to feel important and necessary, like equals. So many ideas have been crushed or forgotten or thrown away because of the fear of confronting the "big bad boss". I have witnessed it firsthand, and it is quite a sad thing. For example, I have a friend who was telling me about an inefficient system at work and how he thinks it could easily be improved and brought up to speed with the rest of the company's efficiency. When I mentioned that he should talk to his boss, he immediately brushed it off and said it would never be implemented, and that it was too hard to talk to the boss anyway. This is precisely why we must never let this be the case- a potential amazing idea was lost that day. But never fear, it doesn't have to happen in your company anytime soon!

CHAPTER 6:

WE ARE NATURAL ENTREPRENEURS

"Everything started as nothing." – Ben Weissenstein, Grand Slam Garage Sales

A major characteristic of Millennials is that we are self-starters and love creating something from nothing. In fact, *30% of us started our own businesses in college,* and *35% of us have started a side business.* That's a lot of entrepreneurs. If you think that's a threatening characteristic for your employees, think again. Some of the top employees and innovators are entrepreneurs, even within companies. Here's why.

CREATIVE AND INNOVATIVE

These are both traits, I'm assuming, that you hope your own employees will possess. Well you're in luck, because many of us grew up with an entrepreneurial mindset, meaning we are primed for these qualities to become part of our lifestyle. This mindset stemmed from the fact that a lot of Millennials are graduating college in a ton of debt with fewer job opportunities than previous generations entering the workforce, and so need to find quick ways to solve the debt in a more efficient way. So, we build companies from the ground up to get us started on tackling this issue more quickly.[8]

In fact, we hope that you will also encourage these same entrepreneurial qualities we are used to in your company, so that we can feel free to exercise our minds and our creative sides while at work. They could be quite good for your company, and might even create some new aspects that make your company the best it's ever been.

WHAT YOU CAN DO:

If, for instance, your company is looking for a solution to a problem you are facing in a certain area, we are naturally inclined to search for an innovative way to solve it. This is mostly because Millennials, as a group, carry a more entrepreneurial mindset as I mentioned before, and one of asking "why not?" instead of just "why?".[9]

Let's say you are looking to solve a market share problem for a division of your pharmaceutical company. Present the problem to a team that you create for this purpose, ask them to collaborate on solutions, and get out of the way. Give some deadlines and guidelines on budget and timing, then let them brainstorm and get back to you with ideas. I guarantee you will be surprised by the results. You will likely not only end up with a more cohesive team of coworkers, but you may also have a plan or two to implement to combat your eroding market share problem.

Be sure to continually give Millennials bigger responsibilities in creating or being a part of something new. We get excited when we can be part of the beginning of something, and thus feel more connected to the project. Plus, our creative juices will start flowing as we figure out ways to make it better, as we now feel it is our responsibility to make it awesome.

WE WON'T (NECESSARILY) LEAVE YOUR COMPANY TO PURSUE OUR OWN

This holds true if you are encouraging and utilizing our entrepreneurial tendencies. Then, we will simply use our entrepreneurial spirit to bring new ideas or aspects *within* your company to life. If we feel as though we can make our mark within the company by starting something, creating something new, we won't feel the urge to leave in order to do so.

FOR EXAMPLE, imagine there's a current sales slump in your restaurant. Let us reach out to coworkers to try and solve the problem ourselves, which will also give you insight into who your best leaders may be by the way they organize groups. You can also observe these groups and understand whose opinions are valued by the leader, and who is not participating and thus might not be vital to your company. We are likely to come up with ideas that will span the scope of the business, but we will be open to prioritizing the solutions and will be sure to present a fiscal picture as well as a gross sales picture so that the final solutions will be well-thought-out and driven by consensus.

Alternatively, we might decide that our sector needs a new "Wow" factor and focus our time on figuring out what could make us really stand out. Remember, we are primed to think differently, because of the job shortage when we first came into the workplace looking for them out of college. We had to find different, unique ways to make a living. Thus, even at your company, we will be trying to *think differently* and think *better*, so as to make the most of our experience, while trying to change the world. I think you'll want this mindset to be encouraged at your office, because we might be able to take the company to new heights with our big ideas.

GIVE US FREEDOM

Or give us nothing at all! Alright, a bit dramatic, but sometimes drama can be a good thing. In order for us to be entrepreneurial and bring the creativity and innovation that we all crave, you need to give us the freedom to work in a flexible environment. If you give us set hours, set tasks, set procedures, and so on…we will find it hard to deviate and thus get stuck in a rut of repetition and stagnation. Deviation is a good thing, so let us know that it is okay to venture off the path and let our minds wander. Chances are you may be an entrepreneur yourself, trying to build your company and wanting to hire the best employees. In this case, even better- you know exactly how it feels to crave the freedom and flexibility to allow our minds to think big things without restraint.

Entrepreneurs do not like being tied down to a certain place, to certain hours, or one certain task. Give us the necessary outputs for the day, week, month, or whatever you decide, and let us get there on our own. Then, we may even come up with a better solution to your plan that we could not have thought of with such strict guidelines and rules. In fact, *77% percent of us claim that having flexible work hours would actually make us more productive at work.*[10]

Consider that before telling us that you don't think we will get enough done if we aren't given a tight schedule and routine to stick to each day.

65% said they felt that rigid hierarchies and outdated management styles failed to get the most out of younger recruits.[11]

Yes, there are some industries that will likely always require set working hours. Think how maddening it would be to get off of a plane only to learn that the baggage handlers decided they wanted to "work from home" today. But even those jobs are ripe for internal scheduling technologies which would allow employees to trade their schedule for another person's schedule when needed or wanted. Nurses, waiters, flight attendants, even delivery personnel could all benefit from simple applications which would keep employers' schedules in real time, but personal schedules could be altered provided another person picks up your slot. It's all about flexibility.

WORK-LIFE BALANCE

Quick side note as we are talking about flexibility in the workplace. We've all heard this before, but now more than ever, young people entering the workforce place more importance on making enough time for family and social life than many generations before them. In fact, a survey conducted by Ernst & Young's Global Generations Research found that **lack of flexibility was cited among the top reasons Millennials quit**

jobs. It gets even worse when starting a family comes into play, as *nearly 40 percent of young workers surveyed in the US are so unhappy with the lack of paid parental-leave policies that they say they would be willing to move to another country.* This is starting to change, slowly but surely, with big tech companies now offering generous parental leave packages for both male and female employees. Take Etsy, for example.

We designed our new parental leave policy to be flexible, gender-blind and to counteract unconscious bias. We want to support and enable parents, regardless of their gender, to play equal roles in building successful companies and nurturing their families. This fits squarely within Etsy's mission to reimagine commerce in ways that build a more fulfilling and lasting world.[12]

The company later cites the generous parental-leave policy as a "competitive necessity" for a company in the tech realm, where so many companies are vying for the top candidates, and are forced to keep up with other countries' policies to keep an edge.[13]

With the known increased focus on proper life balance by Millennials, these bigger companies must adjust their policies to better attract the best of the latest working generation.

We are of course willing to work hard and smart for you and your company. We just don't equate "hard and smart" with time. Sometimes work or a project takes a great deal of time, but sometimes we can accomplish a lot in a short amount of time. We want to control the time factor, but please don't think that means we won't work "hard and smart" for you.

So, keep this in mind when you are restructuring your policies; we place heavier importance on family and balance than previous generations. This balance could be a deal-breaker when it comes to finding the right company to take our talents. I do realize, though, that Gen X before us was also very interested in taking time off to balance work and life properly. However, the difference lies in that Gen X'ers were willing to sacrifice career for this balance, because it had not been appropriately established yet. Remember the "Mommy track"? Millennials expect that companies have caught on by now, as they should, given the amount of times it has been emphasized, and that we should not have to sacrifice any career progress or promotion for the pursuit of this proper life balance.[14]

CASE STUDY: DELOITTE DADS[15]

DELOITTE SAW THE NEED FOR A BETTER WORK-LIFE BALANCE IN THE UPCOMING GENERATIONS AND DID SOMETHING ABOUT IT. DELOITTE DADS IS AN INITIATIVE THAT WAS STARTED BY A JUNIOR CONSULTANT IN THE MANAGEMENT CONSULTING DIVISION IN THE COMPANY'S TORONTO OFFICE.

How:

IT WAS CREATED TO HELP WORKING DADS ACHIEVE A MORE BALANCED LIFE, BY NETWORKING WITH OTHER EXPECTING, NEW, AND VETERAN FATHERS. THE PROGRAM ALSO HELPS THEM ESTABLISH A MORE SUCCESSFUL PHILOSOPHY TO TRANSLATE INTO A HAPPIER LIFE AT WORK AND AT HOME.

WHAT YOU CAN DO:

Mindsets are changing. Now, employers need to adjust to accommodate the Millennials' increased desire to be more involved parents and spouses. Give women *and* men parental leave, and more freedom to take time off to be with their families. It's not just the women who want to raise the kids- more and more men want to be more involved fathers, while their wives continue working after their leave has ended. This should sound very familiar to any Boomers out there; the Boomers were the first generation in which women were more widely expected to go back to work after having children.[16]

Millennials may be the first generation where both men and women are expected to continue working equally after having children, but with more balance. No more 60-80 hour work weeks- we are interested in keeping this balance for both spouses.

"If you listen to the best young male workers, the ones coming out of the top business schools, they all talk about wanting to be really involved fathers, expecting and assuming that their wives are going to be committed to their careers," says Michael Kimmel, a sociology professor at Stony Brook University.[17]

This is a major area where we Millennials differ from the Boomers at this point in our lives, yet are similar to Gen X in a way. Boomers were very focused on achieving the highest point in their careers as quickly as possible, and very motivated by money and prestige.

Because they saw the sometimes negative effects of this extreme work ethic, Gen X strives more for work-life balance and will sacrifice position and salary to find this equilibrium. Gen X wants more work-life balance over higher salary, but they are also more prone to drop out and leave a company rather than stay and engage themselves to eventually move up and grow in their positions. Millennials, similarly, would sacrifice a higher salary in most cases for a better work-life balance overall, but expect that they should not have to and will constantly strive to grow and develop in their careers.[18] They expect that employers will now work to give employees the time off that they need, and the benefits that they need, to create this perfect work-life balance for all employees. And, that this increased focus on the perfect balance will not affect promotions, success, or progress in their careers at all.

CHAPTER 7:
TECH, TECH, TECH

"Millennials don't look at technology as an extra. They expect to be able to use it in all aspects of their lives, including at home, in the community, and on the job. They are becoming a primary consumer and the essential customer at work."[19]

As mentioned earlier, we are the *digital generation*. We need technology. We literally cannot live without it. We are the generation of constant cell phone use, texting, and streaming. If you have not yet incorporated technology into your company, you're going to need to do that before expecting to get any Millennials to come to you and stay with you. Hear me out.

MOBILITY

This is crucial. We can take our devices anywhere, meaning we can do much of our work from anywhere. Many companies that are based online or do much of their work individually have already found that giving employees the opportunity to work from home on some days is huge for increasing productivity and worker happiness. Eliminating a stressful or long commute a few days each week may just prove to be the solution for keeping everyone happy in the long term. Plus, it may even decrease some of your costs if you let employees create their own working environments occasionally. In fact, a whopping *92% of Millennials want to work remote, and 87% want to work on their own schedules.*[20]

Most would choose to have the option to work from home over a higher salary. Instead of separating work life from home life, we are revolutionizing *integration*, mixing our work and home lives so they are in sync with one another. This does not mean that we are always working, even at home. Rather, it means that our lives are more balanced and integrated- we enjoy our jobs and what we learn so do not have to completely shut off when we are "off the clock". We can continue to brainstorm and discover because of our continued interest in the work and can take time at home to work if it is hard to get into the office that day. Integration makes for happier employees. They don't have to live for the weekends because their job offers them the freedom they crave in their busy lives.

SOCIAL MEDIA CLARITY AND ADVANTAGES

Everyone knows we love our social media. Facebook, Instagram, Snapchat, Twitter- the list keeps growing, and we are constantly posting more and more details about our lives. Sure, you might see it as oversharing. But since it is what we know and have grown accustomed to, we have begun to rely on it for news, reviews, recommendations, and pretty much anything we will spend our time doing.

WHAT YOU CAN DO:

In keeping your company and environment attractive to Millennial employees, you will want to understand how much social media matters when we are looking for and deciding on a place to spend the majority of our lives in the coming years. We want a place where we can post about the cool and exciting things our company is doing in the office today, or ask for opinions on an awesome new idea for the office we came up with on our lunch break. Staggering statistics back this up in the real world:

- *1 in 3 Millennials said social media is a higher priority than salary*
- *56% won't even accept a job from a company that bans the use of social media*[21]

If you have restrictions on social media we may feel constrained, causing a bit of dissonance between our reality and the reality you're giving us at work. We need the personal and work life *integration* in more than one area, clearly.

You might be thinking this a silly idea, because wouldn't we all just waste time on social media at work if it were allowed? It's actually been found that productivity *increases by 9%* when allowed to use social media.[21] That's hard to ignore. Give it a try, and see what happens for your company- it could be revolutionary! This all comes with the understanding that social media browsing, scrolling, and posting is not harmful for us as employees during our workday. Because work and life are interconnected for us Millennials, we do not see it as something that impedes our productivity, but something that is required for us to feel 'normal' and balanced at all times. You may see it as "wasting" time while at work to scroll through Facebook or Instagram, but remember that we don't have the "working hours" mindset like the Boomers did. We may get home and remember that we wanted to finish that one thing before tomorrow, and so will work on it at home at 8pm. Boomers could always "turn off" when they left the office at 5pm- they didn't have cell phones, and they could leave their pager in the car. We no longer "turn off" at all and are happy to be connected at all times on our terms. This in itself redefines the concept of working hours as you may know it, and thus changes the concept of productivity as measured in time *at* work.

GET YOUR TECH ON

It's pretty amazing how much we care about the latest tech innovations. So much so that we may even feel more committed and loyal to a company that gives us our own cool tech-y equipment. I have friends who joined their company and got a new Surface Pro or FitBit, and they are so excited about it that they tell everyone. This is an easy, immediate way to spread buzz about your company and get people talking. It may even prompt others to apply just for the sake of being part of a place that's so trendy…so innovative…so generous!

59% said that an employer's provision of state-of-the art technology was important to them when considering a job.[22]

I realize that not every company is big enough or wealthy enough for these costly investments in your employees. Maybe you're on the smaller side and can't afford to give every employee a new tablet or fancy watch for immediate use upon signing. In that case, simply having your products and equipment up to date, and maybe a few things available for company use to fill that tech desire in the office will certainly suffice. Grab a new Oculus VR headset for use in the break room that can transport employees to a country of their choice during lunch, for example. We'll go crazy for that kind of thing.

> HERE'S A LIST OF THE TOP TECHNOLOGICAL INNOVATIONS FOR MILLENNIALS TODAY (WHICH, YOU CAN BE SURE, IS CONSTANTLY CHANGING)[23]

- 3D PRINTER
- SELF-DRIVING CAR
- GOOGLE GLASS
- 3D HOLOGRAPHIC VIDEOS
- OCULUS RIFT

CHAPTER 8:

HEALTH ISN'T JUST PERSONAL

"To keep the body in good health is a duty, otherwise we shall not be able to keep our mind strong and clear." -Buddha

With so many advancements in medicine and new discoveries in healthcare, but also new diseases popping up left and right, more and more of us have had personal experiences with the effects of healthy living on our lives. Like the Boomers, who can be credited with starting the fitness revolution, Millennials love the social aspect but also long-term benefits of regular exercise and healthy eating.

THE ORIGINAL FITNESS GENERATION[24]

BABY BOOMERS LED AN UNPRECEDENTED FITNESS REVOLUTION, INTO A KIND OF GOLDEN ERA OF HEALTH," SAYS KENNETH H. COOPER, M.D.

IN 1984, 54% OF AMERICAN ADULTS EXERCISED REGULARLY, UP FROM JUST 24% IN 1968. THE MID- TO LATE- 80'S WERE THE PRIME OF THE BOOMERS' FITNESS YEARS, WHILE THEY WERE YOUNG AND WORKING. EXERCISE EVOLVED INTO A SOCIAL ACTIVITY, AND ALL-INCLUSIVE HEALTH CLUBS SPRANG UP ALL OVER THE COUNTRY.

While it may seem superfluous to bring this up in a book about the workplace, it is actually a crucial element when it comes to choosing the right place for us to spend our time. Millennials are much more likely to choose a company that supports our personal health and wellbeing over one that does not even have that on the agenda. While we may be earning less overall than previous generations, we are spending more of our income on health and fitness, because we value it above many other aspects in our life.[25]

HEALTH NUTS

To get an idea of what kinds of things you might be able to bring into your company, take a look at what some of the top healthy companies (big and small) are doing to keep their employees happy and healthy. These companies have ranked in the top healthiest companies around the country[26]:

GOOGLE

- Provides on-site nurses and physicians for all employees
- Provides employees physical fitness programs and on-site gyms
- On-site gourmet healthy cafeteria

MICROSOFT

- Environmentally sustainable on-campus cafes and kitchens, "3-star green"

- Flexible work hours and paid gym membership, on-campus spa, sports fields
- Full health package that includes dental, vision, physician house calls, free on-campus health screenings and flu shots

THE WHITEWAVE FOODS CORPORATION (DENVER, CO)

- Gourmet food offerings at on-site café (includes locally-sourced foods- fresh meats and fish)
- On-site fitness classes- yoga, Zumba, Pilates
- Honor system sick policy lets employees take the time they need to recover

RED VENTURES (CHARLOTTE, NC)

- In-house basketball court, yoga studio, bowling alley, and fitness center
- Untracked vacation time lets employees decide how much time off they need to be at the top of their game
- Annual company trip to the Caribbean or Mexico

HONEST TEA (BETHESDA, MD)

- Quarterly Whole Foods gift certificates and weekly organic fresh fruit delivery
- Wellness seminars- stress management, sleep habits, etc.
- Boot camp offered two times a week after work

Companies that support the health and personal wellbeing of their employees create happier, more productive, employees at work.

QUICK FACT CHECK

- WORKERS WHO ATE HEALTHY THE ENTIRE DAY WERE 25 PERCENT MORE LIKELY TO HAVE HIGHER JOB PERFORMANCE.
- WORKERS WHO EXERCISED FOR 30 OR MORE MINUTES THREE OR MORE DAYS A WEEK WERE 15 PERCENT MORE LIKELY TO HAVE HIGHER JOB PERFORMANCE.
- WORKERS WITH WELL-MANAGED CHRONIC DISEASES EXPERIENCE HIGHER PRODUCTIVITY THAN INDIVIDUALS WITHOUT CHRONIC DISEASE WHO ARE OBESE AND DO NOT EXERCISE.
- COMPANIES THAT SUPPORT WORKPLACE HEALTH HAVE A GREATER PERCENTAGE OF EMPLOYEES AT WORK EVERY DAY.[27]

It has been found that those companies that provide gym memberships or health club passes sustain employees for a longer amount of time. In fact, a survey by Monster.com revealed that over *42% of respondents have purposely left a job because of a stressful work environment*, and many of them claim that this has impacted their personal life.[28] Many times, having a stress-relief activity or motivation from work to be active will help to relieve some of the tension that may cause employees to overwork themselves and eventually leave the company.

Specifically, more than half of Millennials say that a healthy work environment is influential to their personal health, compared to only 42% of Gen X and 35% of Boomers. On top of that, when deciding between two otherwise equal jobs, a whopping 96% of us say that great healthcare benefits, like health insurance and dental coverage, would be the most important factor in the final decision.[29]

IN MY EXPERIENCE, MY FRIENDS WHO HAVE RECEIVED A FITBIT THROUGH THEIR WORK, FOR EXAMPLE, HAVE ALMOST IMMEDIATELY SHOWN AN INCREASE IN PHYSICAL HEALTH AWARENESS BECAUSE OF THE PERSONAL GOALS THEY SET FOR THEMSELVES IN TRACKING "STEPS PER DAY".

IT WAS AMAZING TO OBSERVE THAT A SIMPLE ADDITION LIKE THE INCREASED ATTENTION AND CARE FOR YOUR EMPLOYEES' HEALTH WILL CERTAINLY BE APPRECIATED, AND YOU MAY IN TURN SEE AN INCREASE IN LOYALTY AND PRODUCTIVITY AS A RESULT.[30]

CHAPTER 9:
HOW WE WORK

"Working hard and working smart sometimes can be two different things."- Byron Dorgan, former US Senator

Thus far, I've been going on about the innovations to make surrounding the actual work that you do at a company, and how to best understand Millennials. But let's be honest, work is about WORK, and it's what gets done that we all truly care about in the end. You want to either stay a top company or become a top company, and you're learning how to bring in the best people in order to achieve that goal. However, we have not yet gone into depth as far as the actual work that gets done, how it gets done, and what should happen when it gets done. So here we go, let's embark.

TIME VERSUS OUTPUT

Too many companies still do not understand this massive concept that could be the difference between a good worker and a great worker. When you give set hours to get tasks done, or to simply be at work, productivity may in fact decrease.

To capitalize upon the Millennial mindset of efficiency and freedom properly, you will definitely want to consider implementing daily or weekly outputs and goals rather than set hours of work. When we know what we have to finish in a certain amount of time, and the results to show you at the end of it all, we will work harder to get it done quicker, giving us more freedom to work on other things that interest us or simply relax at home. I realize this cannot apply to every job, like those shift jobs that require someone to be at the front desk for a certain amount of time or a cashier at a store whose presence is crucial. But for those of you who have employees in managerial positions or more creative, output-based jobs, this is for you.

IMAGINE an employee with a certain task that can easily be completed in 5 hours, yet it is imposed upon her to be at work at 9am and leave at 5pm. She is clearly going to move very slowly, increase distractions, and become counterproductive if she knows she will have so much extra time to fill. Especially if her next task is not clearly specified. Instead, tell her that the report, analysis, and presentation need to be completed by the end of the week. She will work hard to get all of it done at her own pace, finish early, and have time to work on other things that she is interested in outside of those projects. This method is sure to increase productivity and employee happiness when they are given the opportunity to create their own hours knowing there is a deadline for them to meet.

And, as a bonus, this is also a new way to *monitor* productivity. A manager will be able to see who the productive employees are, the ones getting their work done ahead of schedule, and assign them more work as time goes on. This could potentially lead to faster career advancement for those working quickly and efficiently, whereas those who are struggling to get the week's work done may be brought to the manager's attention as well. Millennials are willing to give the required time to the job that needs to get done, but the "face time" that has previously been seen as a measure of productivity is over.

The first one in and last one out has always been praised in the workplace when it comes to impressing the big boss. Now for Millennials, this barely makes sense. We would rather impress you with the crazy amount of work we completed in an even shorter amount of time.[31] So when we leave earlier than everyone else, see that we have actually done more than everyone else in less time. *Efficiency* may in fact be one of our many generational middle names.

REVIEW US FACE TO FACE...AND OFTEN

We like our feedback in real time, from a real person. Gone are the days of Excel spreadsheets with performance scores from the supervisors. Millennials want face to face feedback as it feels more personal, and thus, we will feel more attached to the improvement or change that comes with it. Once again stemming from our social media attachment, we are used to getting immediate "likes" on a post or picture from our friends. We are accustomed to almost immediate reactions attached to our work or performance, and thus would like to see that reflected where we work. Again this may seem counterintuitive if you see us as the generation attached to our phones and devices. That is why the feedback in person means even more to us, because we know how *easy* it is to simply send a text or an email. Hearing it from you face to face increases our respect and appreciation for you and your time that you gave us to help us improve as employees and as people.

Next time you want to tell your Millennial employee something important, pause before hitting "SEND": 51% of Millennials say they would prefer to communicate with a colleague in person, as opposed to only 19% that prefer email.[32]

WHAT YOU CAN DO:

Make a commitment to give real-time reviews to your Millennial employees consistently and more often so that we will work to impress you and work to change between reviews. Coming from you, we will appreciate the time it took for you to review our work and let us know what to change or continue, and thus we will feel obligated to stay and make those adjustments. In turn, our work will constantly be improving and will impact company performance over time, and all it takes is a few minutes every so often from you, telling us how to be better. The power of even a simple "awesome work!" as you pass by us in the office can do wonders for our mood and happiness at work, and lets us know that you appreciate us and the work we do. We are all about the words of affirmation, people.[33]

Positive coaching is crucial to most any management style. If an employee has a task that could be done better, focus on what they are doing right and how they could improve, rather than telling them what they are doing wrong. This goes for any generation, really, not just us needy Millennials.

HOW WE COMMUNICATE

Communication is clearly crucial in the workplace. Nothing would get done if we couldn't talk to each other, exchange ideas, ask for feedback, etc. However, with the Millennials coming in, while other generations continue to work, it is important to recognize that preferences should be accommodated as far as communication goes. The Boomers may still love quickly typing up an email to tell a coworker about a recent development in the project, while Millennials prefer interpersonal interaction at work.[34]

Yes, this may surprise you, given the stereotypes and our obsession with technology. But when it comes to getting things done and working efficiently, Millennials believe in the power of the spoken word and value face-to-face interactions more than you might naturally expect.

For all of you Boomers out there, never fear. We will of course respond to emails instantly and continue keeping those lines of communications open. We are, of course, accustomed to multi-tasking on the digital communication front, so will not hinder your favorite methods one bit.

Because of the differences in generational preferences, it is important that companies hoping to accommodate all employees take into account the varied types of communication and ensure their continued use.

I think the wisest companies provide as many communication options as possible, both for employees and for customers. I know this can be expensive and complex, but we are in the midst of a multigenerational workplace and customer environment, so this must be done. People have different communication preferences and if you are a company wanting your key messages to be received, you have to provide options, including in-person, phone, email, text, live chat, video and more.[35]

Lindsey Pollak

PUT A RING ON IT

Yeah, that's right. Let's get engaged. According to Entrepreneur Magazine, company engagement is huge when selecting where to take our talents and bright ideas.[36]

A study conducted by the Corporate Executive Board found that employees most committed to their organizations put in 57% more effort and are 87% less likely to resign than employees who consider themselves disengaged.[37]

We want to feel part of something, part of a community, part of something bigger. Employees who felt they had a job that was impacting the greater world are two times more satisfied at work.[38]

WHAT YOU CAN DO:

Part of getting us engaged involves giving us more responsibilities, more interactions throughout the day (whether it be professional or social), or even simple check-ins with coworkers to go over what we've been working on all day. Having events where coworkers get to interact and form friendships is crucial, even if it's something simple like a company Taco Tuesday or happy hour on Thursday. Millennials rely on interaction and social events to feel truly part of something, and feel connected to the place where they work. But remember, it has to be genuine. Don't force your managers to get to know their employees in a social setting like Taco Tuesday if they really don't care. Some will be better at certain things than others, so you could always try different forms of engagement for those less interested in the social situations- say, for example, encouraging a manager to gather notes and feedback from his or her Millennial employees to talk through or review together at work. Don't try to make a person into someone they are not because of the need for engagement, but let your newer Millennial workers mold a workplace that works best for them, while at the same time benefitting your company. Engagement inside and outside of the office is mandatory to keep the best talent in your company over the long haul, however you may choose to do it. So let's go pick out a ring, shall we?!

CHAPTER 10:

WORKPLACE CULTURE AND ENVIRONMENT

"Our number one priority is company culture. Our whole belief is that if you get the culture right, most of the other stuff like delivering great customer service or building a long-term enduring brand will just happen naturally on its own."- Tony Hsieh, CEO, Zappos

Your company culture *is* your company, and it is what customers and clients see when they choose to work with you over someone else. It is crucial, but it is even more crucial that your own employees are comfortable and happy in the culture you have helped to create, or else your company will struggle to hold on to them. As Millennials, we love openness in communication and a laid-back culture, as has been mentioned before. So what does this mean for you?

Make sure we know that you are encouraging employees to be themselves at work- after all, this is the place where we spend the majority of our lives. We want to be comfortable in our own skin at work, and feel accepted for who we are. Some of the best companies for Millennials take this very seriously: they encourage employees to decorate their workspace and make it their own, so that they can truly feel that this is their home away from home. Another idea may be to have one day a week that employees can wear whatever they want, something that lets their true selves shine. Or maybe even encourage different divisions to create "team T-shirts" to wear to foster a sense of unity within your company. If we feel this comfortable and happy at work, that is what we will project. Thus your company will become an extension of the casual, fun culture you encourage.

Culture also extends to how employees interact with one another and the communication that occurs during the workday. It is important to establish this early on, as you don't want anyone coming in feeling that they can't talk to their coworkers or supervisors as easily as they would like to at work. Open up all lines of communication and encourage people to leave their doors and spaces open and welcoming so that ideas can be exchanged at any time. This is an easy way to make us feel more connected and comfortable at work, which seriously improves our performance overall.

Millennials have begun to inspire this idea of the "open office space", stemming from our obsession with openness on all fronts. This idea encourages floor plans to be more open and inclusive, less cubicles and more common areas, less separation and more incorporation. More and more places are catching on, and new services are offering shared working spaces like WeWork and PivotDesk. Some companies, like Microsoft, have even incorporated "free-address" work spaces, with no assigned seating or desks.[39] The openness makes management more approachable, the culture more communicative, and the company more transparent as a whole. Take a look at some things you can incorporate into your business to make it more appealing to the new generation.

HOT DESKING:

THE LATEST CRAZE IN THE OFFICE SPACE INNOVATION ARENA. THIS IS A CONCEPT THAT ALLOWS WORKERS TO SHUFFLE BETWEEN WORKING SPACES, TO SWITCH UP THE SCENERY AND THUS NOT GET STUCK IN A RUT. GONE ARE THE DAYS OF ASSIGNED SEATING; TODAY'S WORKING ENVIRONMENTS PROVIDE FOR MORE COLLABORATION AND DISCUSSION AMONG COWORKERS BECAUSE OF THE FLEXIBILITY AND OPENNESS OF THE SPACE.

LEVEL THE PLAYING FIELD:

BY ENCOURAGING AN OPEN OFFICE SPACE. YOU CAN TAKE THIS QUITE LITERALLY, AND SIMPLY KNOCK OUT ANY WALLS THAT SEPARATE OFFICES OR CUBICLES, AND HAVE EVERYONE SHARE THE SAME LARGE DESK. FACEBOOK SUCCEEDED AT THIS CONCEPT, WHERE THE CEO, HR MANAGER, AND INTERN ALL WORK ON THE SAME DESK IN THE SAME SPACE. COMMUNICATION LINES WILL OPEN UP, AND IDEAS WILL THRIVE, AS THERE IS LESS A FEELING OF HIERARCHY THAT TYPICALLY COMES WITH THE CONCEPT OF THE "CORNER OFFICE". CUBICLES WILL BE A MAJOR

TURN-OFF TO YOUR TOP PROSPECTS UPON VISITING THE OFFICE. CONSIDER SOMETHING LIKE THE PHOTO BELOW, WHERE EMPLOYEES CAN SHARE A DESK AND THUS SHARE A SENSE OF EQUALITY AND COLLABORATION.

FOSTER CREATIVITY AND INNOVATION

"CREATIVE INNOVATION SPACES" CAN GIVE US A PLACE TO EXPLORE OUR IDEAS FREELY WITH WHITEBOARDS SURROUNDING US AND MIND-MAPS ENCOURAGED. [SIDE NOTE: MIND-MAPPING IS USED TO VISUALLY ORGANIZE INFORMATION, SHOWING RELATIONSHIPS AMONG PIECES OF THE WHOLE. IDEAS BRANCH OUT FROM A CENTRAL IDEA, AND IT IS VERY COMMON AMONG MILLENNIAL WORKERS TODAY.] A BREAK FROM THE CONFERENCE OR MEETING

ROOMS WILL HELP US UNWIND AND LET THE CREATIVE JUICES FLOW. REMEMBER, WE ARE THE GENERATION OF COLLABORATION, OF SHARING, OF PEER REVIEWS. THIS MAKES US MORE RECEPTIVE TO THE TEAM MINDSET, AND WE ARE BETTER AT TACKLING PROBLEMS IN A TEAM ENVIRONMENT THAN ON OUR OWN AND ISOLATED. THE OFFICE WHERE WE SPEND OUR DAYS NEEDS TO BE CONDUCIVE TO THIS MINDSET AND THIS WORKING STYLE.

Take this office below for example:

In this office, employees share tables where they work, and face each other at their respective tables. This fosters open communication and ease of collaboration in everyday worklife, which could in turn create a healthier, stronger workplace for all of your employees. They can more easily bounce ideas off of each other and ask for insight or advice anytime.

Sure, the office space and how your desks are arranged is not going to make or break your company, and you might be glazing over this section right now. But you want to know how to keep Millennials engaged and working hard for your company, and this could be a major factor for many of us. The collaborative, cooperative culture achieved with an open environment can foster crucial traits like creativity and innovation, and these are things you don't want to be ignoring in your company culture.

CHAPTER 11:

WE WANT TO CHANGE THE WORLD

"I was raised to believe I could change the world. I'm desperate for you to show me that the work we do here matters, even just a little bit. I'll make copies. I'll fetch coffee. I'll do the grunt work. But I'm not doing it to help you get a new Mercedes.

I'll give you everything I've got, but I need to know it makes a difference to something bigger than your bottom line."[40] Elizabeth McLeod, Millennial

We are big dreamers, innovative thinkers, social changers, with really one goal: to make a change in the world. We want to feel like we have contributed to something meaningful, and really make an **ACTUAL** difference. As opposed to some other generations, Millennials value this value in a workplace, over many other factors like money, location, loyalty, etc. Boomers were the original "make a difference" generation, with the various social, political and civil movements that they incited as young people, so this should all sound very familiar. For example, Boomers ushered in the civil rights movement, and Millennials are cementing the technological revolution, among others. Boomers roused the feminist movement, and Millennials are pushing for marriage equality among all sexualities. Both generations have been key in major revolutionary movements in the country, so have more in common in this aspect than we may think.

The difference comes in our methods of creating change, and the sacrifices we want to make in order to do so. Boomers were all about the protests and physical movements, while Millennials are much less likely to go out on the street and hold up signs in protest. We will post all over Facebook and Twitter to make our points- to spread the word about something we believe in. So while our ways of doing it may differ, Millennials and Boomers clearly share this desire to change the world and make it better for the future.

Because our jobs are where we realize we will be spending much of our lives, we now expect companies we consider working for to have a strong mission and desire to make a difference in the world. If your company does not yet have a social mission or way that you hope to make the world a better place, it might be time to find that missing piece. Dedicate yourself to this, and we will notice even more.

TAKE A LOOK AT THESE MEASURES TO SEE HOW MUCH WE REALLY DO CARE:

- 92% OF MILLENNIALS BELIEVE THAT BUSINESS SHOULD BE MEASURED BY MORE THAN JUST PROFIT AND SHOULD FOCUS ON A SOCIETAL PURPOSE[41]
- 84% GAVE TO CHARITIES IN 2014, AND 78% MADE THESE DONATIONS COMPLETELY ON THEIR OWN, RATHER THAN IT BEING SOLICITED BY THEIR COMPANY
- 59% SAID THEY HAD OR WOULD SEEK OUT AN EMPLOYER WHOSE CORPORATE VALUES MATCHED THEIR OWN

- 45% PARTICIPATED IN A COMPANY-WIDE VOLUNTEER DAY
- 32% USED PAID TIME OFF TO VOLUNTEER
- 16% TOOK UNPAID TIME OFF TO VOLUNTEER[42]

TAKING ACTION:

JEAN CASE, A FORMER EXECUTIVE AT AOL AND CHIEF EXECUTIVE OF THE CASE FOUNDATION, SAYS THAT MILLENNIALS ARE MUCH MORE GENEROUS THAN PEOPLE THINK, REFERRING TO US AS THE "GREAT GENERATION". HE SAYS, "ONE COMMON THEME AMONG ALL YOUNG PEOPLE, IT WAS TRUE OF BABY BOOMERS AND GEN XERS AT THIS AGE - THEY'RE IDEALISTIC. THE BIG DIFFERENCE, WHEN WE BEGAN LOOKING AT MILLENNIALS, IS THAT THEY'RE TURNING THEIR IDEALISM INTO ACTION IN A VERY REAL WAY." RATHER THAN SIMPLY TALKING ABOUT THE CHANGE WE WANT TO MAKE IN THE WORLD, WE ARE ACTUALLY DOING SOMETHING ABOUT IT.

This is an area I can speak to personally, too. When I had the idea for my foundation, DreamCatchers, I immediately started making it happen. It did not cross my mind that it would ever just remain simply an idea, and now it has grown nationally. This mindset is common among my generation, as I have many friends who have started their own volunteer programs, foundations, and even businesses that have a charitable focus or a greater purpose. So next time you hear someone tell you how self-centered we are, how we're going to bring the world down with us, hopefully you can now tell them immediately that they have clearly never truly gotten to know one of us!

KEEP IN MIND:

The percentage of Millennials volunteering through company-wide volunteering events or days is actually lower than previous generations. Hardly any of us are personally motivated by our companies or bosses to get out there and volunteer at company-wide events. We would rather be inspired by our own peers and experiences, and find causes to which we feel a personal connection.

WHAT YOU CAN DO:

My advice to you: don't increase your employee volunteer days. We don't like being "forced" into volunteering because we are already dedicating part of our lives to it outside of work in another way closer to our hearts. Instead, give employees a say in where the company's donations will go, and give us more time off to volunteer. Even giving employees the freedom to go on a service trip has proven to be a great way to increase happiness and retention rates. According to research, a hefty 82% of Millennials surveyed will continue to work at the company that supported their service trip experience.[43]

In fact, the personal growth experienced could even lead to better performance at work. We want to do something that utilizes our skills, something that connects to our passion. And that's something we can find on our own, given the time and support from our company to do so.

But never fear, you can always make sure we are spending that time wisely to ease your mind a bit. Ask us to post on social media about our volunteer experience, service trip, or whatever it may be, and tag your company. This will increase our loyalty to you over time, because we will feel more connected to the company that gave us the freedom to follow our passion for service, in a way that we have chosen. Our friends, families, colleagues, will see these posts, and become even more impressed with your company. My friends who post about their companies on Facebook tend to *continue* to post regularly, and they are the ones that are sure they will stay with their companies for a long time. They are proud to show that their company supports them in their endeavors outside of work, and are sure to recommend you to their high-achieving friends as well. Win-win!

CHAPTER 12:

NOW THAT YOU'VE GOT US, KEEP US

"Your number one customers are your people. Look after employees first and then customers last."- Ian Hutchinson, author

Now that you've taken all the action to make your workplace more attractive to us, you need to start thinking about retention rates. It is a common perception that Millennials "hop around" to companies every year or two. As true as this may be in some instances, it may actually surprise you how loyal we really are, as opposed to previous generations. Consider these stats:

- ✓ 80% of Millennials think they'll work for 4 or less companies throughout their career
- ✓ 36% think they'll stay with their current company for 3-5 years
- ✓ Surprisingly, 16% think they'll stay at their current job for the rest of their career- that's quite a bit considering our reputation![44]

It IS possible to keep a great Millennial with your company for the long term- these statistics back that up.

It is up to you to make your environment conducive to staying over a longer period of time. Many of these were mentioned throughout my book already, but here is a nice shortened list for you to check off as you master them:

CHECK LIST

- PROMOTIONS SHOULD BE MORE FREQUENT- EVEN IF IT'S JUST ADDING NEW LEVELS, "BADGES", OR SOMETHING TO MAKE US THINK WE ARE MOVING UP- IT MIGHT BE THAT SIMPLE
- CONSTANT LEARNING AND PERSONAL DEVELOPMENT MUST BE PRIORITIZED
- FLEXIBLE WORKING HOURS SHOULD BE AN OPTION, FOR THOSE THAT DON'T REQUIRE "SHIFT" WORK
- OCCASIONAL WORKING FROM HOME SHOULD BE AN OPTION, OR SIMPLY WORK MOBILITY
- HEALTHY WORK-LIFE BALANCE MUST BE MAINTAINED AND ENCOURAGED
- TRY FOR A MORE OPEN WORK ENVIRONMENT WITH FLEXIBLE DESKS, OPEN AND CREATIVE SPACES, WINDOWS, AND MOVEMENT
- EMPHASIZE YOUR GREATER PURPOSE, GREATER MISSION, AND HOW YOUR COMPANY IMPACTS THE WORLD
- ALLOW EMPLOYEES FREE VOLUNTEER DAYS TO USE WHERE THEY WISH
- ENSURE ALL FORMS OF COMMUNICATION ARE INTACT AND ACTIVE, AND SOCIAL MEDIA IS VISIBLE

If you are able to check off most of these items on the list above, you are certainly well on your way to becoming a top company for Millennials. And, you are sure to *keep* us if you continue to implement these strategies effectively and consistently. To really give you hope, I have called upon one of my Millennial friends, also from my class at Notre Dame. Colleen Wade is surely a "top Millennial" due to her diligence at work and her commitment to changing the world for the better. Read on for her story about her journey to finding Abbott, and be inspired to make some changes to similarly impact your employees in the long run.

COLLEEN WADE, IT ANALYST, ABBOTT LABORATORIES

When I was looking for an internship for the summer after my junior year of college, I knew I was looking for **something different**. I'd spent the previous summer researching microfinance in Uganda and came away from that service learning experience knowing I wanted to pursue a career in social impact/**entrepreneurship**. The only problem was that I was majoring in IT Management. My professor advised me to spend my next summer internship using my IT skills in a corporate setting, giving me the chance to apply what I was learning in a challenging yet structured environment. I trusted her advice and decided that if I was going to go the corporate route, it needed to be with a company that was **making a positive impact in the world**. This made it easy to cross off some of the more prestigious IT consulting companies. I wanted to know that I was working for a **socially conscious company** each day, regardless of the "client" I was placed on.

My older sister advised me to look at **Abbott** after her company worked with Abbott on a social project in India. She made the argument that larger corporations are actually the ones **driving a lot of social change** around the world. I started looking into Abbott and researching their **corporate social**

responsibility initiatives. I was shocked by how strategic and aligned they were with their core competencies (i.e. healthcare product development). **They were doing much more than an "employee day of volunteering" or giving millions of dollars in donations**. In addition to those purely philanthropic efforts, they were working with local farmers in Haiti to design, source and manufacture a nutrition product in-country that met the needs of malnourished children in the area. They were truly using their presence and strength in emerging markets to **improve people's lives** through the products they offered. I was no longer interested in any other companies, **regardless of their perceived prestige or paychecks**. I jumped full force into my interviews with Abbott and was given the opportunity to intern with them the summer before my senior year.

At then end of my internship, I was offered a position in Abbott's IT Professional Development Program following graduation and I absolutely wanted to take it. The company had lived up to my altruistic expectations and I truly believed that we were helping people around the world live life to the fullest. The only thing holding me back was that I desperately wanted to have the experience of working for a social enterprise first. A mentor of mine suggested that I take as much time as I could after graduation to pursue this goal. So, I had to ask my Abbott recruiter if I could push back my start date, which might mess with the rotation program dates. My recruiter's immediate answer to my request was that **this desire to work for social impact** was the reason they wanted to hire me. **She had no problem pushing the date back** with the understanding that I would start within 6 months of the original date. This was more time that I had expected and could not have been happier. In my eyes, it also was a litmus test for **how truly socially conscious the company was. By supporting my personal dream of working for a social enterprise, Abbott proved to me that they didn't just value me for my GPA or IT skills - they shared my motivation to create a brighter future for the world and develop my professional skills in various work environments, no matter how non-traditional.**

My experience in the Professional Development Program (PDP) has confirmed this fact time and time again. I have an open-ended 5% annual performance goal related specifically to development – **I meet monthly with my mentor, set personal development goals and work on projects of my choice outside of my assignment responsibilities.** Some of the side projects I've most enjoyed in the last year have been speaking at a summit on Millennials in the workforce, starting a Young Professionals Employee Network at the company and working on projects for the Global Citizenship organization. I've also had the chance to **practice management skills** in the PDP committees I'm involved with - another 5% annual performance goal.

While this may sound like a lot in addition to my day-to-day responsibilities, **I'm motivated to volunteer for additional projects because I believe in this company and its mission.** I believe in the values that it stands for and the people I'm working alongside. **I feel like I am the best version of myself when I'm at work and that the people around me support me and my goals.**

It sounds crazy coming from a Millennial, but I have no interest in switching companies anytime soon. Like many of my colleagues, I see myself spending my career at Abbott and making a positive impact in the world as a result.

If that doesn't make you excited to implement some of these strategies, I'm not sure what will! Colleen is a prime example of a Millennial who was *attracted* to her company for its social mission, and is actually planning on *staying* for her entire career because of its commitment to her personal growth and social change. And I know that you can be next, with a few simple updates, changes, and the new knowledge that you have now.

To give you a taste of other Millennial-successful companies, I have interviewed two companies who ranked in Fortune's 100 Best Workplaces for Millennials. *Read on for their take on how to keep your company attractive to Millennials, and why you should be working hard to get the most out of the new generations.*

INTERVIEW WITH KELLI VALADE, PRESIDENT OF CHILI'S GRILL AND BAR

Chili's Grill and Bar was ranked #11 on Fortune's 100 Best Workplaces for Millennials. The President of Chili's, Kelli Valade, tells us how they got there and how they intend to stay there.

TELL US ABOUT CHILI'S WORKPLACE CULTURE.

Chili's is a brand steeped in heritage, but revitalized into a young brand with a fun, lively, spirited culture. We encourage personalities and our employees' whole selves to come to work each day. For example, we will have T-shirt contests where employees can decorate their shirts to showcase their personalities. This allows them to stand out, while also encouraging a fun, open environment in the workplace. Our motto is "Once a Chili-head, always a Chili-head", meaning you are forever part of the Chili's family once you start; it becomes part of your fiber.

When employees start, we immediately figure out why they work, and what is most important to them in a career. We strive to incorporate the Gallup 5 elements of well-being into their jobs- financial, career, social, community, and physical. We have specific programs for each of these elements, and want employees to bring their entire selves to their job, so we make that easy for them to keep a healthy balance. Chili's gives them a family to take care of them if they ever need it.

SPEAKING OF A HEALTHY BALANCE, HOW DO YOU ENSURE THAT EMPLOYEE'S KEEP A WORK-LIFE BALANCE?

With Chili's, a work-life balance is in the nature of the restaurant business. The hourly members naturally have a work life of flexibility- they have a say in their schedules and can work when they are available. We conduct a panel session to ensure that we achieve balance in the 5 areas mentioned above, and keep employees whole in each area. For example, we can help physically with assistance in meal and food prep, through programs designed to teach employees how to cook and eat better foods. There are naturally more hours in this business, but we focus on keeping our employees whole and happy, to ensure that they are bringing their best selves, and whole selves, to work. We design a 5-day work week in most cases, but we also try to get creative in how we address the work-life balance.

TELL US ABOUT HOW YOU HELP EMPLOYEES DEVELOP AND MOVE UP WITHIN YOUR COMPANY.

Sure; there is a host of opportunities for our employees to grow within the company. The typical path is from server, to key team member, to manager, within our restaurants. In fact, about 45% of our managers come from the team member ranks. We also have a lot of restaurants that open each year, even internationally. We encourage members to help a restaurant open, either locally or beyond, so they are able to grow and learn in their positions by being involved in an opening. Moving from manager to general manager, and above, is encouraged and assisted through our specific events to bring in the leaders in the company. Employees can move throughout the company laterally or straight up the ladder. Our home office has more opportunity for moving around on different projects, and we do our best to encourage team projects to keep employees challenged and engaged. We will usually take our best leaders from around the company and put them on a problem, to push and test their skills on a team. This helps them to think strategically, and develop their knowledge and skills within the company, and with their colleagues.

WHAT IS YOUR OFFICE LAYOUT AND PHYSICAL STRUCTURE LIKE?

If you were to come to our home office, you would walk around the space and see that it is very highly branded by our restaurant. You immediately know you are in a restaurant space- there are pictures of food everywhere, a timeline of our history, meeting rooms named after our restaurants. One of our meeting rooms is designed based on the first Chili's ever, and each element in that room is a reference to that first restaurant.

We have a very spirited culture, so there are photos everywhere of our team doing things together, during and outside of work. Some of our employees have whiteboards at their desks, and give them a personal touch. I can tell a lot about our employees based on their personal décor and what they write on their whiteboards each day. It is very clear in our office that personalities matter, and we encourage them to come out.

As far as dress code, we are very informal. In fact, my jeans have holes in them right now.

WHAT IS YOUR STANCE ON COMMUNITY SERVICE- IS IT ENCOURAGED AT CHILI'S? HOW?

Of course. Our company is a big supporter of St. Jude's Children's Hospital, which started with our restaurants in Memphis. They were interested in doing more to support the local hospital, so they started the campaign which has now become a huge part of our company. Our restaurants do everything to decide how they will support, and our amazing guests give so much to make it happen. We don't dictate what each restaurant has to do each year, but rather have a position called "Hope Captains" who bring ideas to us. They decide how we will collect money each year, and how we can better engage in service in each community.

Other than that, we encourage employees to get involved in the community around food initiatives- volunteering at food banks, for example. Our employees do some amazing work on their own, but team building events are also encouraged within the company. Because of flexibility in schedules, employees can sign up for time off to do these events and engage in service, and sometimes we will even encourage them with paid time off specifically for volunteer work.

TELL US ABOUT YOUR SOCIAL MEDIA POLICIES AT WORK.

We love social media. In fact, we encourage it. We even have specific social media training at the general manager conferences each year. We want employees to share their voices, because each voice is very important to us. We have over 75,000 team members- each member is an ambassador for Chili's who we want to share his or her own stories. Being present in the social space is crucial, and our social media outlets are full of amazing stories to create an amazing experience for our guests. Our policies are very liberal, and we love to keep it very organic, with very real employee and guest stories.

HOW DO YOU ENCOURAGE HEALTH IN THE WORKPLACE?

We are always testing things that are new out there, to stay on top. We have a place in every office where there are healthy snacks for everyone. We offer a variety of different things to teach people to be healthy, too. We have yoga classes, boot camps, a culinary center, and even occasionally bring in programs like WeightWatchers to encourage employee health.

WHY IS IT IMPORTANT TO YOU, AS PRESIDENT, TO HAVE MILLENNIALS AND ENSURE EACH GENERATION IS REPRESENTED PROPERLY WITHIN YOUR COMPANY?

It is very important to me personally, because I believe that diversity in thinking and skills and attitudes is critical. The next generation will always bring a new perspective. As a mother of two, I have Gen Z children (generation after Millennials), who think they are going to change the world. It's fantastic. I recently watched a panel of Millennials saying how they want someone to connect with them, challenge them, inspire them, unleash them. If we can do that for Millennials, with all different characteristics, we will create a great company for everyone. We want to tap into as many Millennials as we can today, to make the best company possible.

We are also starting something called **Millennials Council**. Since we are a fairly large company, we want to know how to feel connected to a bigger vision and purpose. The council will consist of 70 Millennials, who will travel and have live meetings with me, we will Facebook chat and blog together, and they will tell me about their lives. I want to get to know them personally, so I can begin to see things through their eyes. I want to find ways to make it feel small here, to engage everyone. I want to take this generation and learn as much from them as possible.

INTERVIEW WITH CHRISTINE TRAVIS, GLOBAL PUBLIC RELATIONS MANAGER AT ADROLL

AdRoll

AdRoll is a global technology company that offers advertisers retargeting products for cross-platform, cross-device display advertising. Christine Travis is a Millennial who has been with the company for 1 year.

WHAT MADE YOU INTERESTED IN WORKING AT ADROLL?

I think it really appealed to me because right off the bat, our CEO said he wants employees to work there not to join something great, but to *build* something great. It gives us a sense of ownership, allows us to get our hands dirty and take on opportunities to grow the brand.

WHY DO YOU THINK THE COMPANY WAS NAMED IN THE TOP WORKPLACES FOR MILLENNIALS?

We live and breathe *culture*. Our core values come alive in spirit animals, which represent each company value in a living form. We highlight them each year. For example, one of our company spirit animals is a jellyfish, representing the complete transparency we strive for in the company. We want everyone to be comfortable asking anything and everything, and we have regular company-wide meetings where we can submit questions anonymously in case we are afraid to ask them. The CEO then goes through them all and answers every single one; he likes to consider it a way to "flush the toxins" from the company, instead of letting issues fester and grow.

HOW DOES ADROLL ENCOURAGE PERSONAL DEVELOPMENT?

Training and development within the company is huge. We realize that if an employee is not getting the training and development they are looking for, they will simply move on. Our training program is robust; mentors and teachers come in often for training, and we hold courses to help employees grow personally as well as professionally. For example, we have a coding course for non-engineers, and a session where our CEO mentors employees, explaining how he got to where he is and how other employees can create a similar pathway for themselves. We want everyone to feel as though they are getting the most out of their time with the company.

WHAT IS THE WORKPLACE LAYOUT LIKE? HOW DO PEOPLE WORK?

The office is entirely an open layout; we do not have any cubicles or offices. The CEO, CFO, and entry level employees all share the same area, the same table tops. This fosters a very open, collaborative environment, which makes people communicate a lot more. There is no such thing as a "closed door policy", because there aren't any offices, and therefore no doors that can be closed.

TELL US ABOUT THE MOBILITY AND FLEXIBILITY THAT EMPLOYEES HAVE AT ADROLL.

It differs across teams, but we are pretty flexible. For example, the engineering team can be mobile and work from anywhere. Gmail and Slack allow us to communicate openly at all times during the workday, and there are plenty of ways to check in on what is happening within the company or your division any time.

IS WORK-LIFE BALANCE A BIG THING FOR ADROLL?

It is extremely important, and that comes from the top. Our CEO is a father of two, so he understands the importance of family, and that is reflected in that the company really focuses on our individual interests and what we spend our time on outside of work. We have ample time off, and we have lots of fun things to encourage taking a break from work- a company soccer team, a wine club, and other groups where employees can interact outside of work. That brings me back to another spirit animal of the company- the monkey. It reminds us to take work seriously, but not ourselves.

WHAT IS ADROLL'S INVOLVEMENT IN THE COMMUNITY?

The company is hugely focused on community; in 2009 we founded AdRoll Gives Back, a local volunteering effort with an annual goal for hours spent within the company devoted to the community. Last year we surpassed 3000 hours, through initiatives like serving at the food bank, Habitat for Humanity, and other causes that are close to our employees' hearts. We want to do right by the customer and the community, and mostly focus our volunteer efforts on education, professional development, and community support.

IS THERE ANY SORT OF FOCUS ON KEEPING A HEALTHY LIFESTYLE AT ADROLL?

Yes, there are various perks that the company offers employees like medical and dental benefits, wellness classes, and a health subsidy for using on a gym membership or promoting a healthy lifestyle. There are always healthy snacks in the office, so there is a big focus on nourishing yourself well while working.

IS TRAVELING AND WORKING FROM ABROAD AN OPTION?

Absolutely. We have over 500 employees now, with offices in San Francisco, London, Dublin, Tokyo, Sydney, and New York. AdRoll has an open door policy for employees, meaning you are allowed to work out of any office, anywhere. This encourages employees to travel and meet other international employees, expanding their network and scope.

WHAT ARE THE SOCIAL MEDIA POLICIES, IF ANY, AT ADROLL?

Social media is always encouraged, and we are on all platforms. We recognize that it is crucial to engage on social media, and be featured in the top 20 feeds so that others can understand what we are all about.

IS THERE ANYTHING YOU WOULD LIKE TO ADD ABOUT YOUR PERSONAL EXPERIENCE WITH THE COMPANY, OR ANY OTHER POINTS?

Sure. I really love working at AdRoll because it gives me the opportunity to drive new initiatives forward, sharpen my skills, and develop myself personally with internal classes and new opportunities. AdRoll understands that work isn't really all about work, but rather it is important to focus on the employees, and focus on opportunities within the community. The company gets that it is crucial to understand the individual and his or her whole self, their goals, and how each person focuses and drives their career.

FINAL NOTES

All this talk about Millennials really just boils down to one thing, always a force to be reckoned with in the world: the **power of youth**. Every generation moves through their young years in a different way, making different marks, and changing the world in different areas. Young people have a way of thinking, hoping, dreaming, and *doing* like no other age group, because they are still young enough to dream big, yet old enough to actually do something about it. Millennials are a special generation, sure, but we are also similar to every other generation before us- our youth years are full of possibility and the desire for learning and development. We have the world before us, and a life ahead of us, and are ready to conquer anything. Capitalizing upon this very real power of the youthful way of thinking and engaging that is now present in the Millennial generation could make all the difference in building a strong, powerful, and committed company. Take advantage of the presence of youthful Millennials at your company today, and build a better company for the future.

Notes:

---

[1] http://www.census.gov/newsroom/press-releases/2015/cb15-113.html
[2] http://www.huffingtonpost.com/visualnewscom/Millennials-crave-a-workp_b_4613390.html
[3] http://www.avoka.com/blog/2016-Millennial-banking-trends/
[4] http://www.Millennialmarketing.com/wp-content/uploads/2015/03/Maximizing-Millennials-IG-1.jpg
[5] http://knowledge.wharton.upenn.edu/article/how-ge-builds-global-leaders-a-conversation-with-chief-learning-officer-susan-peters/
[6] https://www.pwc.com/gx/en/managing-tomorrows-people/future-of-work/assets/reshaping-the-workplace.pdf
[7] http://99u.com/articles/14709/why-baby-boomers-and-Millennials-make-great-teams
[8] https://www.americanexpress.com/us/small-business/openforum/articles/why-Millennials-could-be-the-most-entrepreneurial-generation-ever/
[9] http://blogs.wsj.com/experts/2015/10/28/why-Millennials-are-the-c-suites-secret-weapon-for-innovation/
[10] http://www.bentley.edu/newsroom/latest-headlines/mind-of-Millennial)
[11] https://www.pwc.com/gx/en/managing-tomorrows-people/future-of-work/assets/reshaping-the-workplace.pdf
[12] https://blog.etsy.com/news/2016/strong-families-strong-business-a-step-forward-in-parental-leave-at-etsy/
[13] http://www.theatlantic.com/business/archive/2016/03/tech-paid-paternity-leave/473922/
[14] https://www.washingtonpost.com/local/Millennials-want-a-work-life-balance-their-bosses-just-dont-get-why/2015/05/05/1859369e-f376-11e4-84a6-6d7c67c50db0_story.html
[15] http://www2.deloitte.com/ca/en/pages/careers/articles/diversity-and-inclusion.html#
[16] http://www.wmfc.org/uploads/GenerationalDifferencesChart.pdf
[17] http://www.bloomberg.com/news/articles/2013-05-30/alpha-dads-men-get-serious-about-work-life-balance
[18] http://smallbiztrends.com/2015/06/Millennials-want-work-life-balance.html
[19] http://fortune.com/2015/08/18/how-tech-savvy-Millennials-are-humanizing-your-workplace/
[20] http://www.forbes.com/sites/danschawbel/2013/12/16/10-ways-Millennials-are-creating-the-future-of-work/#37c065261a59
[21] https://www.tinypulse.com/blog/its-ok-let-gen-y-use-social-media-atwork

[22] https://www.pwc.com/gx/en/managing-tomorrows-people/future-of-work/assets/reshaping-the-workplace.pdf
[23] http://blog.lab42.com/Millennials-technology
[24] http://www.aarp.org/health/healthy-living/info-2014/baby-boomers-fitness-revolution.html
[25] http://www.womensmarketing.com/blog/2015/09/the-Millennial-approach-to-health-wellness/
[26] http://greatist.com/health/healthiest-companies
[27] http://exactmarket.com/healthy-employees-are-happy-employees-and-most-importantly-productive-ones/
[28] http://www.monster.com/about/a/Dangerously-Stressful-Work-Environments-Force-Workers-to-Seek-New-Empl4162014-D3126696
[29] http://www.bentley.edu/newsroom/latest-headlines/mind-of-Millennial
[30] http://fitforwork.org/employer/benefits-of-a-healthy-workforce/
[31] http://www.lifehack.org/articles/productivity/5-productivity-lessons-from-the-Millennial-work-style.html
[32] http://www.bentley.edu/newsroom/latest-headlines/mind-of-Millennial
[33] http://www.forbes.com/sites/danschawbel/2013/12/16/10-ways-Millennials-are-creating-the-future-of-work/2/#4d47cd7f1270
[34] http://www.cio.com/article/3082775/unified-communications/Millennials-are-shaking-up-workplace-communication.html
[35] https://powermore.dell.com/business/Millennials-are-changing-the-workplace/
[36] https://www.entrepreneur.com/article/273191
[37] Corporate Executive Board, The Role of Employee Engagement in the Return to Growth, Bloomberg Businessweek, August 2010
[38] http://www.fastcompany.com/3033488/hit-the-ground-running/4-employee-engagement-secrets-from-Millennials
[39] http://www.forbes.com/sites/neilhowe/2015/03/31/open-offices-back-in-vogue-thanks-to-Millennials/#42415cab4ed1
[40] http://www.mcleodandmore.com/2015/10/13/why-Millennials-dump-their-boss/
[41] https://www.washingtonpost.com/news/wonk/wp/2015/06/24/Millennials-are-actually-more-generous-than-anybody-realizes/
[42] http://www.forbes.com/sites/karlmoore/2014/10/02/Millennials-work-for-purpose-not-paycheck/#9598ff15a225
[43] http://new.www.huffingtonpost.com/mark-horoszowski/when-companies-send-their_b_8365830.html
[44] http://www.bentley.edu/newsroom/latest-headlines/mind-of-Millennial

ABOUT THE AUTHOR

Caitlin Crommett is a recent graduate of the University of Notre Dame and currently resides in Los Angeles. As a typical multitasking Millennial, she freelances as a film producer and actor, occasionally walks dogs and caters events, runs a nonprofit foundation, and of course, speaks and consults on Millennials in the workplace. She hopes to help companies change the way they think about incoming generations, and encourage flexibility and progress in the workplace. Caitlin is also very passionate about generational connection, as her nonprofit also serves to bridge the generational gap between youth and elderly through wish-granting. Check it out at www.DreamCatchers1.org. Thanks for reading!

www.ingramcontent.com/pod-product-compliance
Lightning Source LLC
Chambersburg PA
CBHW071706040426
42446CB00011B/1936